Contents

First published in Great Britain in 2008 byPenhaligon's Friends

© Compiled by Alice Allsworth RN, Cert Ed. & Wendy Ball PCET
© Illustrations & Design by Jenny Nightingale www.jennynightingale.co.uk

Introduction

A child can live through anything so long as he or she is told the truth and is allowed to share the natural feelings people have when they are suffering.
(Eda La Shan)

Following the death of a loved one you may experience a bewildering array of emotions and feelings. In the midst of all that is going on you also have to deal with the ongoing practical and emotional needs of your children.

Just when you need to give the most may be when you have least to offer. You may be struggling with traumatic events surrounding the death and often some very practical pressing changes in your circumstances.

Lots of people will want to tell you what to do meaning to be helpful, but this can sometimes be confusing and sometimes hurtful.

This book is intended to help you by giving you ideas about how to include and involve your children in all that is going on. No one is pretending that it will always be easy but children will react quickly to what is going on around them.

Remember you are your children's most precious resource and you need to look after yourself for their benefit as well as your own. We hope this booklet will help you to navigate your journey and provide useful signposts along the way.

First Thoughts

For parents and carers supporting bereaved children

* It is helpful if you can talk to your children honestly and explain what has happened in a way they can understand. They need information and reassurance.

* Try to talk to your children about the funeral, including them and giving them choices will help them remember and say goodbye.

* Talk often about the person who's died – include your children in remembering.

* How children grieve will depend on their age and their understanding of events.

* Your children's grief may be shown in behaviour and they may be distraught one minute and playing happily the next.

* Inform the school about your children's loss.

* Trust your instincts as a parent and don't be afraid to ask for help if you need it.

* It's OK for you and your children to feel sad, angry, confused, empty, guilty, anxious and many other emotions – and it's OK if you don't.

Early Days - Practical Ideas

* Children often regress into behaviour from an earlier age, don't worry about this. Allow them time to regain their confidence and energy.

* Most children will usually respond well to physical comfort. Cuddles and hugs will help soothe distress and reassure them that you are there for them.

* Snuggling into a fleecy blanket or an extra one on top of them can help.

* Special foods that they like or soft foods from earlier times can be very reassuring.

* Shock can make children (and adults) feel cold and they may need extra layers of clothing. This creates a feeling of being lovingly wrapped and of being protected.

* A radio or tape can be played softly if getting to sleep is difficult.

* If your child is afraid of the dark a nightlight helps.

* Physical play can help children get their feelings out and relieve their anxiety and stress through moving about.

* Grief can make children very tired. Try to plan some quiet time into the day and arrange earlier bedtimes for the children where possible.

* If your child is overeating try offering them a cuddle. If they aren't interested in food try offering them small nourishing meals.

* Keep normal routines going as much as possible. This helps children feel more secure and can give them and you a much needed break.

* You can reduce your children's anxiety about being separated from you by telling them when you are going to be away from them, and when you are coming back.

* Helping your child make a memory box with photos, stories, poems and mementoes is a valuable family activity and gives them permission to talk about the person who's died.

When Someone Has Died by Suicide

Bereavement by suicide is one of the most complicated and painful kinds of bereavement a family can experience. Shock, guilt, anger and sadness are strong emotions which are often accompanied by shame and stigma over this type of death. Intrusive media interest and having to deal with the police and the coroner add to the particular difficulties with this type of bereavement.

What and how to tell the children about the death is one of the most worrying things for a parent to face; it feels as if it would be easier not to explain exactly what has happened. However, children may hear something from other people at school or in the community and then lose their trust in you for not being truthful. Whilst it is important to be honest with children it is also helpful to avoid unnecessary details.

* When someone has died through suicide the process of breaking bad news is the same as for any death. It is just as important in these circumstances to be honest with the children and tell them that their special person has died - followed by **how** they died.
* This can be done in stages and does not have to happen all in one go.
* If children are not told that someone has died through suicide they may hear from others and not be able to discuss their feelings openly.
* Children cope better when they know the truth even though it is often difficult to tell them.

Suicide Resource:

Winston's Wish offer one of the most comprehensive resources available to help parents and carers with supporting children after suicide. They provide a helpful booklet "Beyond the Rough Rock" which can assist adults when telling children how the person died. www.winstonswish.org.uk

Breaking Bad News
To Children

Bad news is best given as soon as possible by someone who knows the child well with support of family, friends or professionals.

1. GET READY

* Know the facts because children will ask
* Find a quiet place without too many interruptions
* Choose a time when the adults are going to be around for a while - e.g. at a weekend
* Have someone around who can support you

2. ASK QUESTIONS TO FIND OUT WHAT THEY KNOW

3. GIVE A WARNING SHOT – "I have some sad news to tell you."

4. EXPLAIN IN STEPS

"You know Dad is in hospital? The doctors have found he has an illness. The illness is called cancer. Cancer is a serious illness and the doctors are not always able to make it better although they are going to try."

5. ANSWER CHILDREN'S QUESTIONS AT THEIR OWN PACE

6. BREAK THE BAD NEWS

7. ALLOW CHILDREN TO EXPRESS FEELINGS

8. ALLOW TIME FOR QUESTIONS AND ANSWER THEM HONESTLY

9. GIVE THE INFORMATION REPEATEDLY OVER A PERIOD OF TIME

Children & Funerals

Should children attend funerals?

The death of a loved one can be a very confusing and challenging experience for a child. Attendance at the funeral can help the child understand the finality of death, and allows them to share the emotional experience with the rest of the family. No child is too young to view a body or attend a funeral, provided that they have been prepared and lovingly guided through the process of what will happen and the things they will see. If children are excluded they may think that death and grief are too horrible to be faced and can feel isolated and frightened. Give the child the choice and include them whenever possible with activities such as:

* Choosing the coffin
* Placing a note, drawing, special object or memento in the coffin
* Picking special songs, music, readings

Preparing children for viewing the body and attending the funeral

Should the children view the body?

This is a frequently asked question and there are no right or wrong answers in the sense that this is an individual choice you make as parents and carers. Seeing the body of the person who's died can help children understand the reality of the death and enable them to say goodbye in a private setting. Be guided by the funeral director and offer children the opportunity. Children should have the chance to share adults' grieving rituals but should feel comfortable with whatever choices are made.

Viewing the body:

You can ask your funeral director if they are able to provide a special viewing of the body for your children. They are often happy to explain to children what happens before and after a funeral. You may find it easier to take children to visit the mortuary, chapel of rest or church ahead of time if possible. Reassure them that they don't have to stay there the whole time if they don't want to and can go outside with an adult to play or go for a walk.

You need to help your children understand:

* What **death** is.
* That the **funeral director** will go to the hospital or home to pick up the body.
* That the body will be taken to the chapel of rest to be kept until it is buried or cremated and will be made ready for them to see (bathed, dressed, hair combed, makeup applied).
* What a **coffin** is, and what it looks like: "A special box that holds the body, made of wood, with handles and a lid. The inside looks a bit like a bed with a pillow."
* What the children will see in the viewing room.
* That they can touch the person or the coffin if they want to.
* They can draw pictures and put things in the coffin.

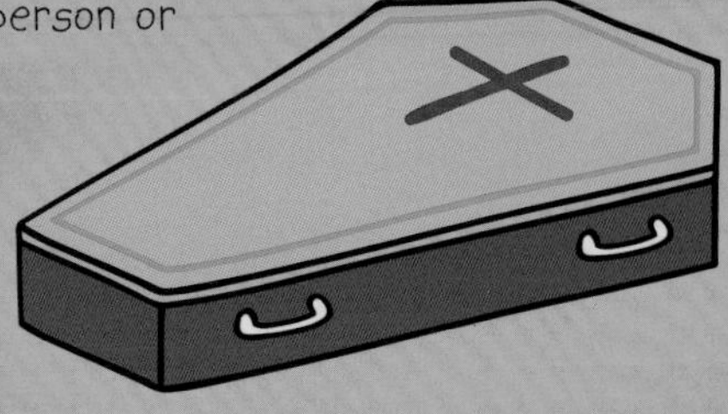

Children & Funerals (continued)

The Funeral

It is helpful to explain the reason for the funeral:

* "We all join together with family and friends in order to remember the person who died."
* "We want to surround them with our love and say goodbye."
* "It is a special time to celebrate the person's life."

Children need to know **what** will happen, **when** and **where** the service will take place, **who** will be there and **why** they are doing things:

Tell them where the funeral service will be held (crematorium, church, at the grave-side) and that it may include hymns, scripture readings, a short sermon, prayers for the person who has died, and **eulogies** (speeches) about the person's life.

Children need to be prepared for seeing adults expressing a wide variety of feelings, including laughter as well as tears, and reassured that any and all of these feelings are okay

After the service, everyone will gather at the family home or some other location to share memories, laugh and cry with others who knew the special person.

If a child doesn't want to attend

It's important to give children the choice of going to the funeral or memorial service but if they don't want to go they shouldn't be forced. Make sure that they don't feel guilty for not attending and tell them that you are happy to talk whenever they are ready.

If they don't go you could:

* Take pictures and make them available whenever they want to see them.
* Make a video or tape recording of the proceedings.
* Write an account of the service: who was there, what happened, who said what.

If you are too upset to support your child at the funeral

Tell your child that you may be upset at the funeral and that someone else close to them will be there to look after them as well. Constant reassurance that all these feelings are natural will help.

It is good to make contingency plans for the funeral service. A family member or close friend who knows the children could be asked to sit with them and care for them, as needed. Someone could sit behind or near the end of their row, so they can leave the service unobtrusively and go outside with them if they become too restless or distressed.

Children & Funerals (continued)

Ideas for explaining Burial

The coffin is taken to the cemetery in a **hearse** (a special car that carries the coffin with the dead body).

Everyone follows in a **funeral procession** (a quiet parade of cars) to the **cemetery** (where dead people are buried).

Everyone gathers around the **grave** (a special hole that's already been dug in the ground) and words and prayers are spoken. Sometimes the coffin is lowered into the grave and family members will gently throw handfuls of dirt or flowers on top.

Later a **grave stone** (a stone or marker) is placed at the grave to mark the place where the body is buried: It tells --------- name, birthday, date of death, and maybe a special saying or poem in loving memory.

Later when we visit the cemetery, we can go to the grave to remember and feel close to ------------, because the love we have for each other continues to live on, even after our special person has died.

Ideas for explaining cremation

Cremation takes place in a special building called a **crematorium**. In this building there is a room with a special fire – not like any room in our house, and not like the fire in our fireplace.

Because ------- is dead, they will not feel anything at all during cremation. A body without life cannot feel heat or pain.

This special fire is very, very hot – hot enough to burn the body and turn it into very fine, very soft ash.

What is left of a dead body is called **ashes.** The ashes may be put into a small container called an **urn**. The urn may be buried in the ground or placed in a special building, or the ashes may be scattered in a beautiful place, such as in the sea or in a garden.

Children's Reaction to Death

Remember Me Always

Children react differently according to their age and understanding but the following are some of the common reactions which may occur:

* Anger or aggressive behaviour to you or their friends or toys
* Tantrums
* Acting out the loss through play
* Clingy and anxious about leaving you
* Wetting the bed and thumb-sucking
* Not sleeping or having bad dreams
* Wanting to share your bed
* Being irritable or restless
* Difficulty concentrating
* Problems with schoolwork
* Regressing in their behaviour, acting like a younger child
* Acting more like an adult
* Crying or giggling for no obvious reason
* Changes in eating habits
* Repetitive behaviour including asking questions over and over again
* Running away or not wanting to go to school
* Mimicking the behaviour of the dead person
* Attention seeking
* Sad or withdrawn

This is not an exhaustive list and if you are at all concerned about any of your children's behaviour there is a useful list of contacts on page 23.

The Effect on the Family

When a family member dies, it will affect the way the family functions as a whole. All the relationships within the family may shift, adjusting to this change in the family structure. Children may mourn the person who died and the environment in the family that existed before the death.

Death of a parent

* Often a child's first thought is that they want their parent back, but they know that they can't make this happen. They may show these feelings with explosive bursts of emotion or negative behaviour.
* It is common for children to blame themselves for their parent's death and they need to be reassured that they are not to blame in any way.
* In the early days they may feel comforted by sleeping in their parent's bed.
* If the relationship with the parent who died was difficult, the child may have very mixed feelings. There may be unresolved issues and they may be left with feelings of pain and rejection, without the opportunity to somehow "make it right". Part of their grieving process will include the pain of never knowing the answers to the questions that are the most significant to them.
* Children can often blame the remaining parent for the death. They may idealise the dead parent and become quite hostile to the surviving parent
* Children frequently worry that their remaining parent or another person close to them may die or leave them and will be concerned about who will take care of them.

The Effect on the Family (continued)

Remember Me Always

One 4 year old girl became whiny and clingy after her father died. Occasionally, she sat in his chair with many blankets wrapped around her.
When she began complaining of stomach aches, her mother took her to the doctor, and she promptly asked him when she could see her father again.
Three months later, she was able to say, "Daddy died."

Death of a sibling

* Siblings may worry about their own safety and possible death.
* Many younger siblings have an extremely difficult time when they reach the age at which their sibling died.
* Older siblings may be plagued by guilt by not "looking out" for their younger brother or sister.
* Some siblings may attempt to take over the identity of the deceased child in order to ease their parents' grief.
* If the relationship was difficult they may fantasise that they caused their sibling's death, (that the good child died and the bad one survived).
* If parents idealise the dead sibling the surviving child can feel jealous, angry, and devalued.
* The death of a twin or triplet can have its own traumas. They may genuinely feel they have lost not only a brother or sister but also a part of themselves.

Grandparents

* The death of a grandparent is likely to be one of the first experiences your child will have of a death in the family.
* How your child reacts will depend on their age and the emotional closeness of the relationship. If your child had a very close relationship with their grandparents and this deep, trusting relationship is suddenly ended by death, it will deprive your child of an important dimension in their life.
* If grandparents were the 'head of the family' it may then be a struggle for the family unit to redefine itself. Sometimes the family won't get together as often and the children don't see their extended family as much as they did before. This can add to the child's sense of loss.

Navigating the Journey over Time

There is no set amount of time that it takes for your children or you to be able to move on with life. It takes as long as it takes but eventually you will find that the pain of grief will ease with the passing of time. The memories will still be there as you all seek to re-adjust to your lives with your loved one missing.

It is helpful to remember a few things as you all move forward on your grief journey. You can help your children by;

Keeping Boundaries

Children respond better to knowing their limits with behaviour and routines. This helps restore their sense of security which has often been badly shaken by their loss.

* Patience and kindness but firm structures help them to know you love them but want the best for them.
* Giving them time and space to express their feelings and allowing them to still be children will help.
* Encourage them to take their share of responsibilities at home without overburdening them.

Building Self Esteem

Your child's self esteem may have been affected by their loss. You can boost this by offering them praise and compliments when it's deserved.

* Show interest in their school work, their friends and outside activities.
* Listen when they want to talk to you.

* Give them as much individual attention as you can.
* Spend time with them, especially at night.
* Hugs and cuddles are some of the most healing ways to restore your child's sense of worth.
* Your children need to know how important they are to you.

Encouragement about the Future

Children may feel despair about life and withdraw from activities.

* Encourage them to play and enjoy life as this can help them to start looking towards the future.
* Explain about the changes that may have to take place because of the death in a positive way. This can lessen their anxiety.
* They may need very clear information and schedules to begin with until they are able to move on with their lives under their own steam.
* Give them choices where possible and include them in family decisions about the future.
* Explain how you are all still a family even if the shape of the family has changed, and that you are working together to try and overcome the grief.
* Give your children permission to be happy again, that it's okay to laugh, play, learn and love.

Looking After Yourself

In order to support your children well you need to find a way of supporting and caring for yourself. It is important to look after the whole of you, including your physical, emotional, social and spiritual needs.

Physically

Whilst you are grieving your eating and sleeping patterns will probably be upset. You can look after yourself by trying to eat healthily and get enough rest, even if you cannot sleep.

If tension or anger affect you it can help to take more physical exercise, even household tasks like gardening or re-decorating can be very therapeutic.

Bereavement can make you feel overwhelmingly tired and you may need to take longer periods of rest, especially in the early months. You may have to ask for extra help from family and friends to look after the children so that you can take a break.

Socially and Emotionally

While you are grieving you may not feel very sociable. Try not to cut yourself off too much from other people as your children might feel more isolated. Perhaps just see one friend or only a few people regularly. This will help you not to depend completely on your children for company.

Friends may not know how best to support you; help them by giving them some ideas about what brings you the most comfort. You may find it helps to have someone that will either just sit with you and not say much, talk about normal things, or who will go for walks.

It will help your child to know that you have other sources of support. You may find it difficult to talk to your family or friends about your grief but there are organisations which provide counselling support for bereaved people. (see Page 23)

Other Ways to Express Your Grief

You may find it helps to express your grief in creative ways i.e. writing, painting or music. Some people find that music can either soothe them or help bring the emotions right to the surface to be expressed through tears or words. Writing and painting can be a healing way of expressing grief and may help you see how far you have come.

Looking After Yourself (continued)

Spiritually

Grief often leads us to question why this death has happened. Most of us have feelings, concerns or needs which relate to our deepest sense of who we are. Even if we don't have a formal religious belief, these beliefs can be called spiritual.

When you are mourning you may choose to explore such concerns with the support of a counsellor whose training encompasses such issues. Religious organisations can be a great source of support, either in the form of individual support, attendance at services or exploration through reading.

Rituals as a Source of Healing

All sorts of rituals can have a deep and healing effect. You may have your own rituals as part of your religion or cultural tradition. If you have no particular religious association you may find comfort through devising your own rituals - perhaps regularly lighting a candle and just sitting quietly, thinking of the person who died, or spending time each week in a 'special' place - perhaps by the grave.

The Solace of Beauty

Another way of spiritual healing is being in contact with natural beauty, preferably in the open air. Time by the sea, in the countryside or park, or sitting in a beautiful building can really help.

> **'Remember that 'super parents' don't exist.
> Just do what you can, when you can.
> Be gentle on yourself.'**
>
> (Winston's Wish)

Where to Get Help

The organisations listed below offer specialist support and some have interactive websites that are designed especially for bereaved young people.

Childhood Bereavement Network
A national network working with bereaved children and young people, their families and caregivers, that offers an online directory of services available nationally.
www.childhoodbereavementnetwork.org.uk

Childline
National helpline for children with any kind of problem or difficulty.
www.childline.co.uk

CRUSE
Bereavement care for adults.
www.crusebereavementcare.org.uk

Merry Widow
A website for anyone who has lost a partner. There are helpful survival guides and a message board to share thoughts and feelings.
www.merrywidow.me.uk

Papyrus
A website to help young people who may be suicidal.
www.papyrus-uk.org

Where to Get Help (continued)

Parentline Plus
A very helpful parenting website with lots of useful links.
www.parentlineplus.org.uk

RD4U
Website especially for young people, interactive, managed by CRUSE.
www.rd4u.org.uk

Survivors of Bereavement by Suicide
www.uk-sobs.org.uk

The Compassionate Friends
Organisation to support parents who have lost a child of any age.
www.tcf.org.uk

The Way Foundation
Organisation to support young widows.
www.wayfoundation.org.uk

Also helpful - To stop unwanted direct mail to those who have died.
www.the-bereavement-register.org.uk

Helpful Books
for Children & their Carers

Beyond the Rough Rocks, Winston's Wish
ISBN: 978-0953912339
Offers practical advice for families in the immediate days and weeks after suicide has been the cause of death.

Dear Grandma Bunny, Bruna D
ISBN: 978-1405219013
A wonderfully simple explanation for young children about death, funerals and feelings.

Help for the Hard Times, Hipp E
ISBN: 978-1568380858
Exploration of various losses that teenagers may be facing in their lives. Written in the appropriate language and well illustrated for this age-group.

I Miss You, Thomas P
ISBN: 978-0764117640
A first look at death.

Josh, Jeffs S & Thomas J
ISBN: 978-1841014234
Coming to terms with the death of a friend.

Muddles Puddles & Sunshine, Winston's Wish
ISBN: 978-1869890582
Helpful series of activities and exercises to help children remember the person who has died and express their feelings.

Helpful Books
for Children & their Carers
(continued)

Remember Me Always

Mudge, Gill and Steve, Dainty J
ISBN: 978-0715148877
The story covers the questions children tend to ask: Why God allows children (and others) to die; what a funeral is and what happens after death?

Remember Me, Penhaligon's Friends
ISBN: 978-0-9550757-0-4
Guidance for schools/educational settings when dealing with childhood loss, bereavement and critical incidents.

Remember Me Too, Penhaligon's Friends
ISBN: 978-0-9550757-1-1
Handbook for busy health care professionals when supporting children.

Samantha Jane's Missing Smile, Kaplow J & Pincus D
ISBN: 978-1591478096
A story about coping with the loss of a parent.

Straight Talk about Death for Teenagers, Grollman E
ISBN: 978-0807025017
Teenagers express their feelings through poems and talk of their own experience.

Waterbugs and Dragonflies, Stickney D
ISBN: 978-08298162420
This children's book explains the Christian belief of life after death through a story about the lifecycle of waterbugs and dragonflies.

We Were Gonna have a Baby We Had An Angel Instead, Schweibert P

ISBN: 978-0972424110

A book to help very young children cope with the death of a sibling before birth, at birth or shortly after birth

What on Earth Do You Do When Someone Dies?, Romain T

ISBN: 978-1575420554

In simple, honest words describes the strong, confusing feelings triggered by death and suggests ways to feel better.

When a Friend Dies, Grootman ME

ISBN: 978-1575421704

Speaks directly and simply to anyone who has suffered the loss of a friend, particularly teenagers

When Someone Very Special Has Died, Heegard M

ISBN: 978-0962050206

A practical format for children to understand the concepts of death and develop coping skills for life. Children illustrate & personalise their loss through art.

Where's Molly Now?, Penhaligon's Friends

ISBN: 978-0-9550757-2-8

Handbook for clergy and pastoral staff when supporting children.

Bibliography

Bowlby, J. (1980) Attachment and Loss: Harper Collins. New York.

Dyregrov, A. (1992) Grief in Children: Jessica Kingsley Publishers.

Elliot, Pat. (1997) Coping with Loss - for parents: Piccadilly Press.

For Parents Supporting Bereaved Children Postcard: Childhood Bereavement Network in Association with Penhaligon's Friends (2006)

Grollman EA. (1990) Talking about death: Beacon Press, Boston

Kroen, William C. (1996) Helping Children Cope with the Loss of a Loved One, A Guide for Grownups: Free Spirit Publishing

LeShan, EJ. (1987) When a Parent Is Very Sick: Macmillan.

Wass, H. Corr, CA (1984) Childhood and Death: Hemisphere Publishing Corporation.

Worden, JW. (1996) Children and Grief: The Guildford Press. New York.

This bereavement guide is supported by:

Ecclesiastical

Ecclesiastical is a specialist insurer providing advice and protection to those people and organisations who care about the communities and environments in which they live and work. They insure and protect the charity, faith, heritage, education and care sector as well as providing personal insurances and financial advice. Ecclesiastical believes that helping bereavement support is an essential part of its corporate social responsibility.

SEIB

South Essex Insurance Brokers Ltd (SEIB) has been providing specialist insurance solutions to the funeral industry since 1963. The Company's reputation has been built on giving good honest advice and they see the bereavement guides as an integral part of their public support.

NAFD

NAFD is the country's leading funeral trade association; their members conduct more than 80% of funerals in the UK. It is in keeping with their caring profession that they are supporting the bereavement guide initiative.

Perfect Choice Funeral Plans

Perfect Choice Funeral Plans are offered by accredited NAFD members and enable individuals to make sure their future wishes are known and carried out and relieve the burden on loved ones at such a distressing time. They see bereavement support as a fundamental part of their business.

Supported by

With the compliments of

in partnership with Perfect Choice Funeral Plans

ISBN 978-0-9550757-3-5